SUPER EASY SONGBOOK

ISBN 978-1-70515-780-0

Cover image © Getty Images / Gareth Cattermole / Staff

Visit Hal Leonard Online at
www.halleonard.com

World headquarters, contact:
Hal Leonard
7777 West Bluemound Road
Milwaukee, WI 53213
Email: info@halleonard.com

In Europe, contact:
Hal Leonard Europe Limited
42 Wigmore Street
Marylebone, London, W1U 2RN
Email: info@halleonardeurope.com

In Australia, contact:
Hal Leonard Australia Pty. Ltd.
4 Lentara Court
Cheltenham, Victoria, 3192 Australia
Email: info@halleonard.com.au

Welcome to the *Super Easy Songbook* series!

This unique collection will help you play your favorite songs quickly and easily. Here's how it works:

- Play the simplified melody with your right hand. Letter names appear inside each note to assist you.

- There are no key signatures to worry about! If a sharp ♯ or flat ♭ is needed, it is shown beside the note each time.

- There are no page turns, so your hands never have to leave the keyboard.

- If two notes are connected by a tie ⌣, hold the first note for the combined number of beats. (The second note does not show a letter name since it is not re-struck.)

- Add basic chords with your left hand using the provided keyboard diagrams. Chord voicings have been carefully chosen to minimize hand movement.

- The left-hand rhythm is up to you, and chord notes can be played together or separately. Be creative!

- If the chords sound muddy, move your left hand an octave* higher. If this gets in the way of playing the melody, move your right hand an octave higher as well.

  * *An octave spans eight notes. If your starting note is C, the next C to the right is an octave higher.*

ALSO AVAILABLE

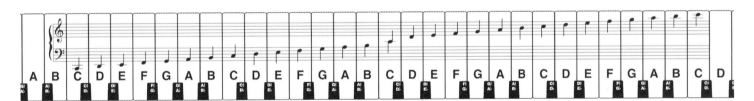

Hal Leonard Student Keyboard Guide HL00296039

Key Stickers HL00100016

All I Ask

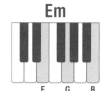 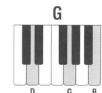 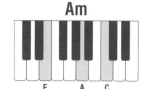 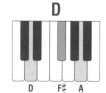 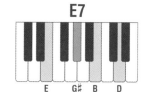

Words and Music by Adele Adkins,
Bruno Mars, Chris Brown
and Philip Lawrence

Can I Get It

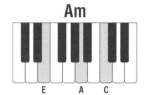
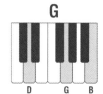
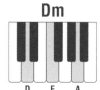
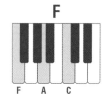

Words and Music by Adele Adkins,
Shellback and Max Martin

Moderately

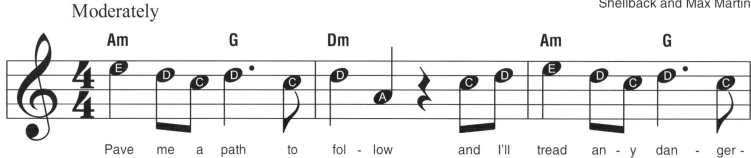

Pave me a path to fol - low and I'll tread an - y dan - ger -

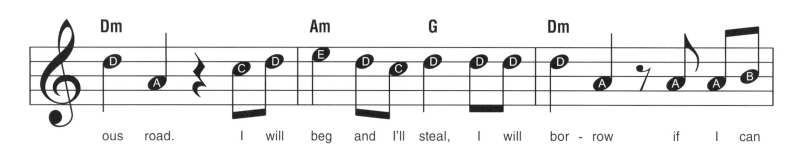

ous road. I will beg and I'll steal, I will bor - row if I can

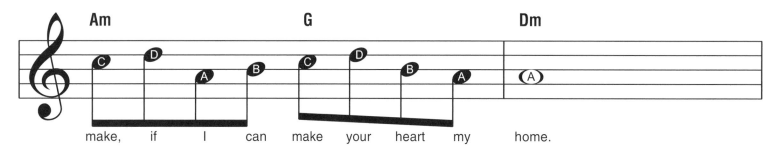

make, if I can make your heart my home.

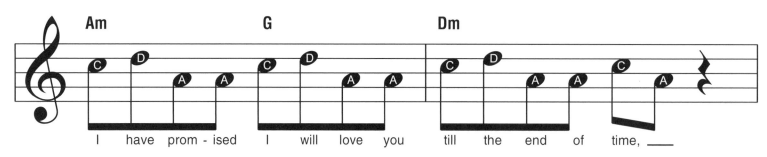

I have prom - ised I will love you till the end of time, ___

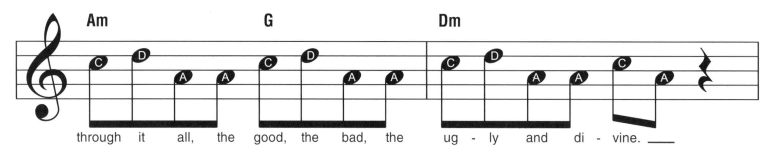

through it all, the good, the bad, the ug - ly and di - vine. ___

Chasing Pavements

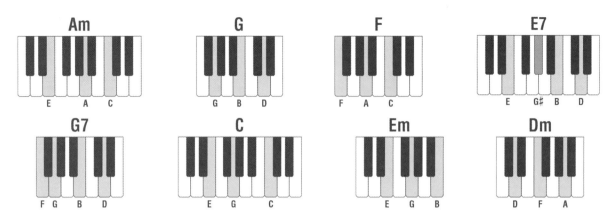

Words and Music by Adele Adkins
and Francis Eg White

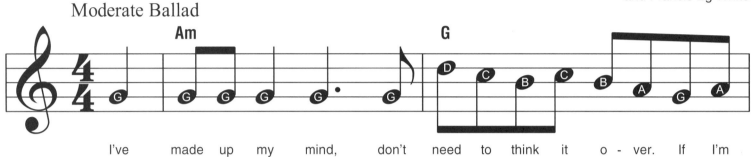

I've made up my mind, don't need to think it o - ver. If I'm

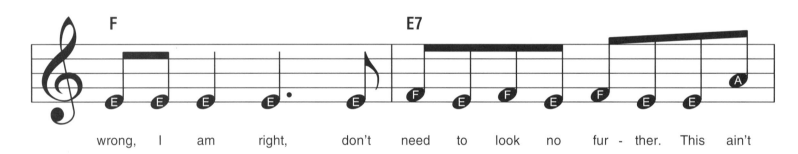

wrong, I am right, don't need to look no fur - ther. This ain't

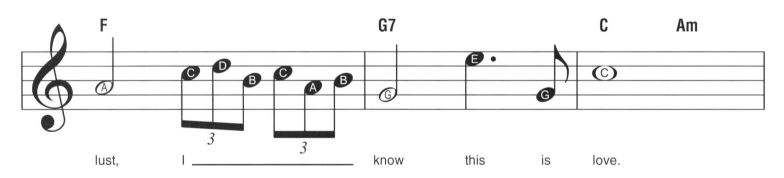

lust, I _____ know this is love.

But if I tell the world, I'll nev - er say e - nough, 'cause it was

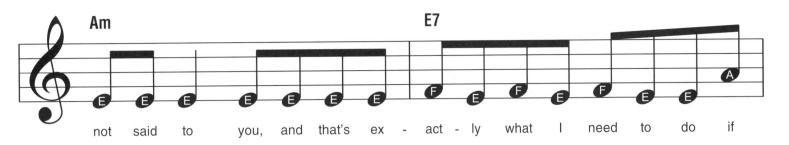

not said to you, and that's ex - act - ly what I need to do if

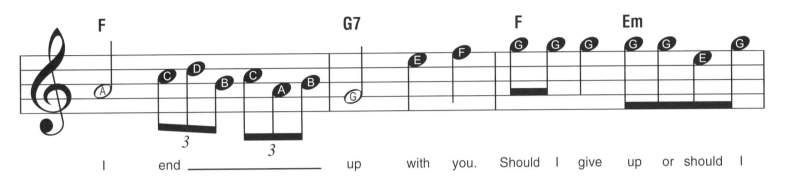

I end _____ up with you. Should I give up or should I

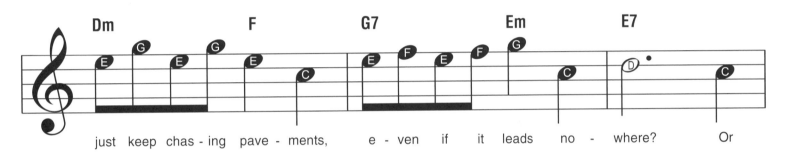

just keep chas - ing pave - ments, e - ven if it leads no - where? Or

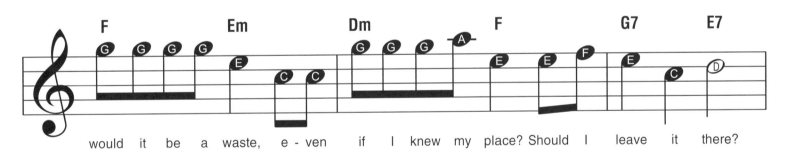

would it be a waste, e - ven if I knew my place? Should I leave it there?

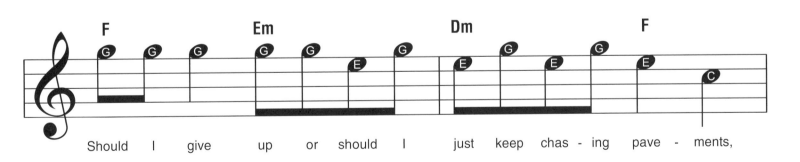

Should I give up or should I just keep chas - ing pave - ments,

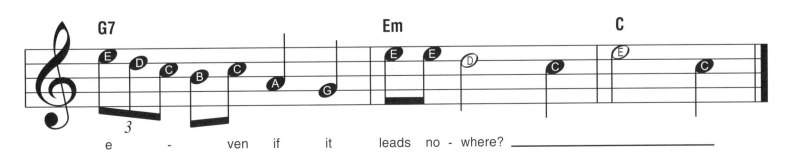

e - ven if it leads no - where? _____

Cold Shoulder

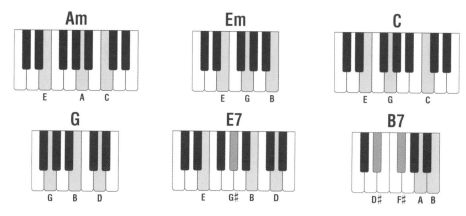

Words and Music by Adele Adkins
and Sacha Skarbek

Moderate Funk Rock

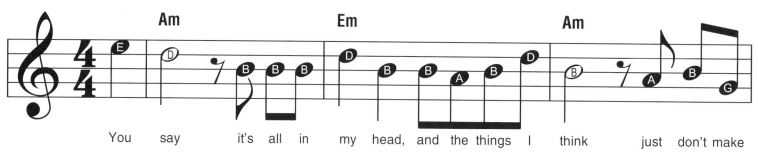

You say it's all in my head, and the things I think just don't make

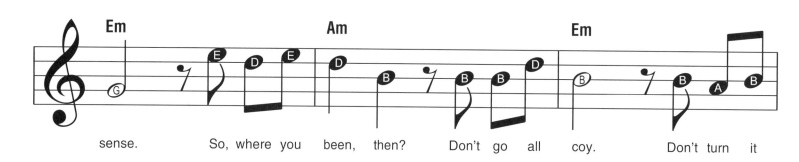

sense. So, where you been, then? Don't go all coy. Don't turn it

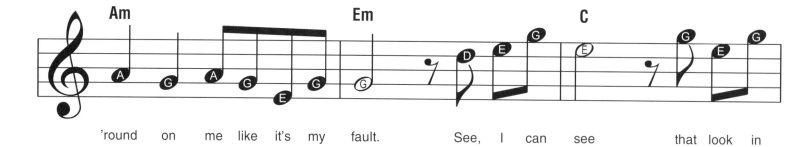

'round on me like it's my fault. See, I can see that look in

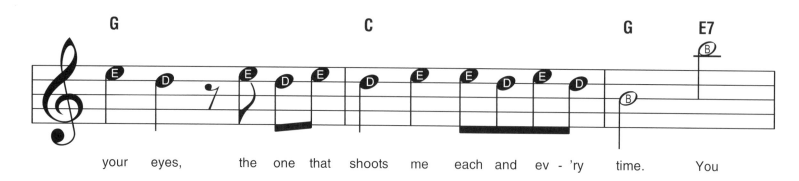

your eyes, the one that shoots me each and ev-'ry time. You

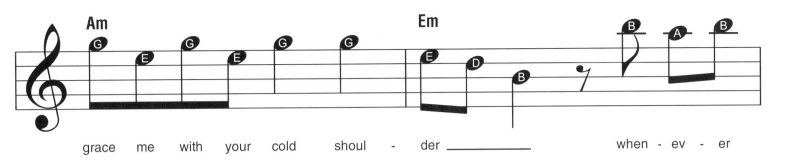

grace me with your cold shoul - der _____ when - ev - er

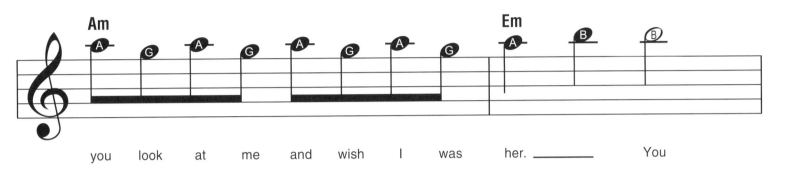

you look at me and wish I was her. _____ You

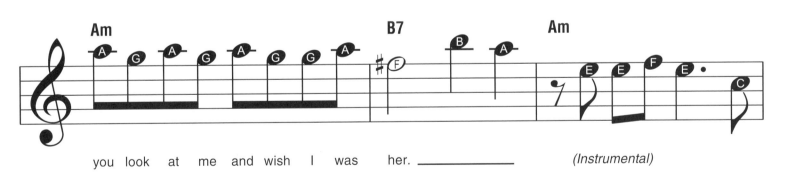

show - er me with words made of knives when - ev - er

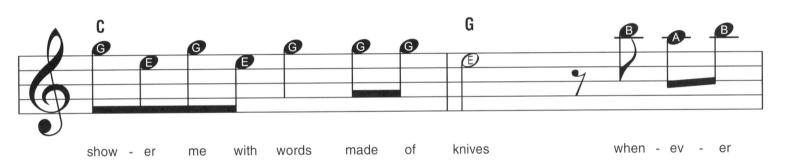

you look at me and wish I was her. _____ (Instrumental)

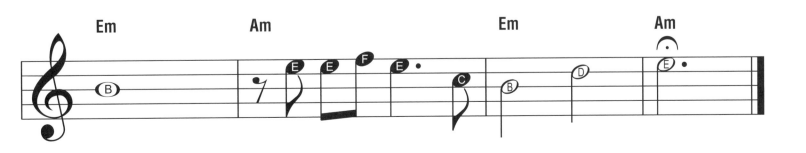

Cry Your Heart Out

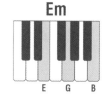
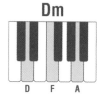

Words and Music by Adele Adkins
and Greg Kurstin

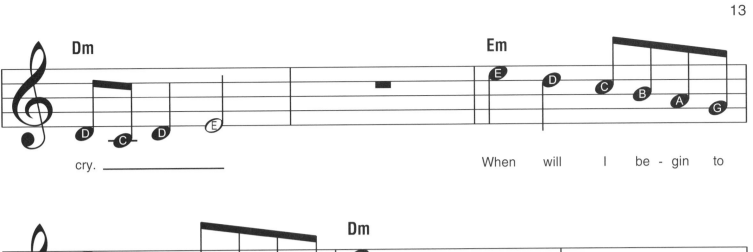

cry. _____ When will I be - gin to

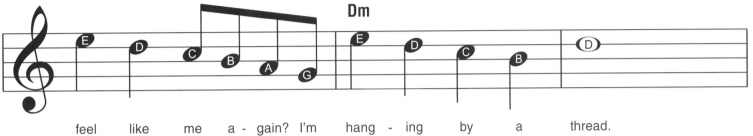

feel like me a - gain? I'm hang - ing by a thread.

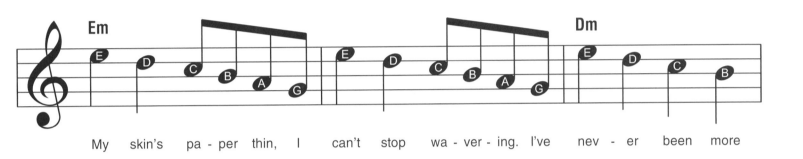

My skin's pa - per thin, I can't stop wa - ver - ing. I've nev - er been more

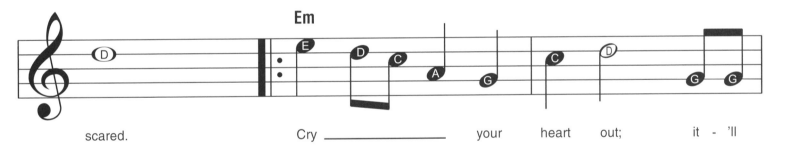

scared. Cry _____ your heart out; it - 'll

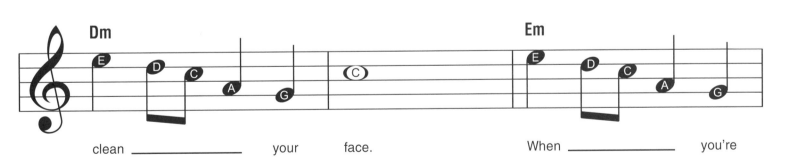

clean _____ your face. When _____ you're

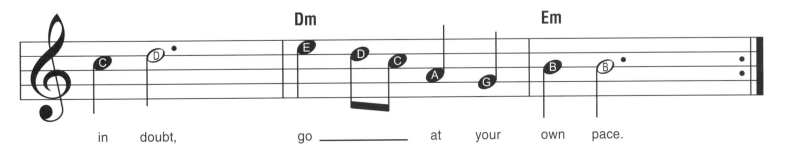

in doubt, go _____ at your own pace.

Easy on Me

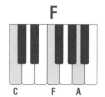
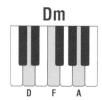
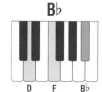
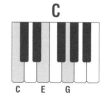

Words and Music by Adele Adkins
and Greg Kurstin

Moderate half-time feel

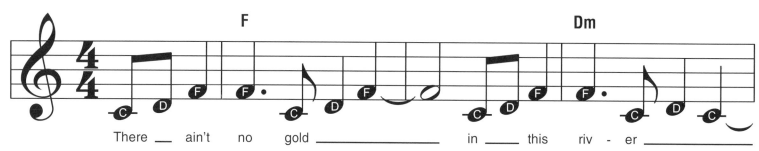

There __ ain't no gold _____ in ___ this riv - er _____

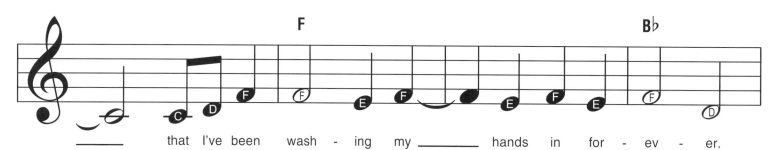

_____ that I've been wash - ing my _____ hands in for - ev - er.

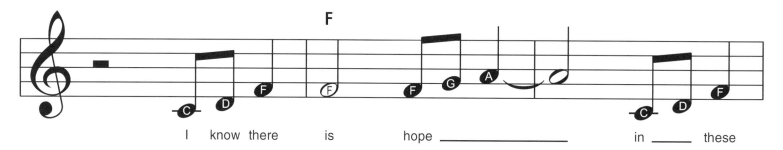

I know there is hope _____ in ___ these

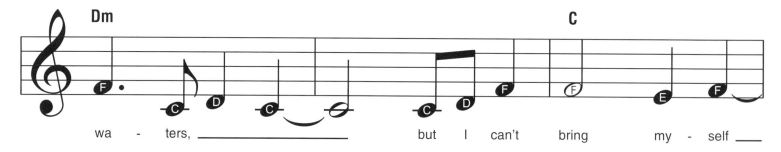

wa - ters, _____ but I can't bring my - self ___

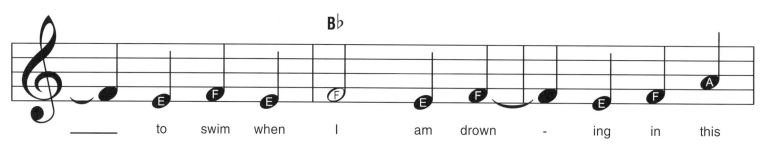

_____ to swim when I am drown - ing in this

Hello

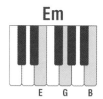
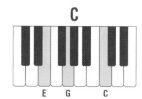
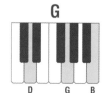
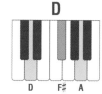

Words and Music by Adele Adkins
and Greg Kurstin

Moderately slow

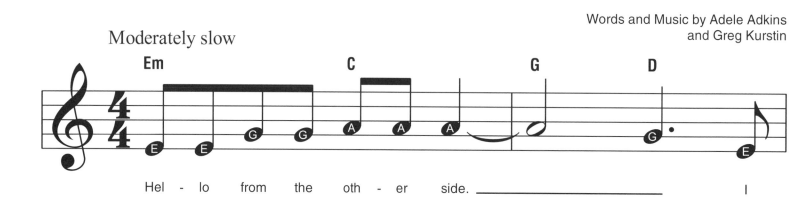

Hel - lo from the oth - er side. _____ I

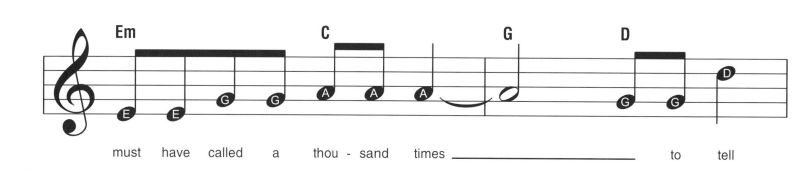

must have called a thou - sand times _____ to tell

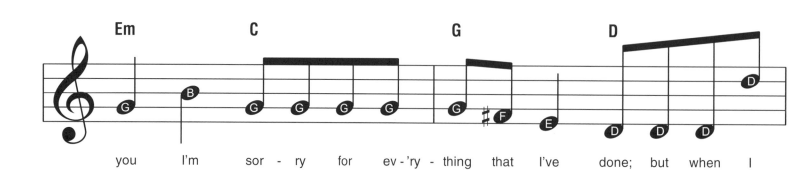

you I'm sor - ry for ev - 'ry - thing that I've done; but when I

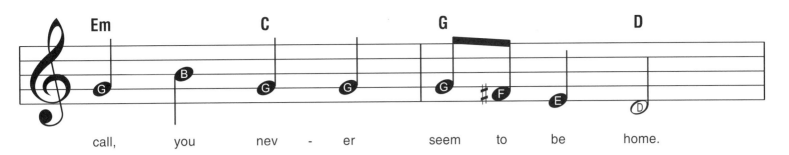

call, you nev - er seem to be home.

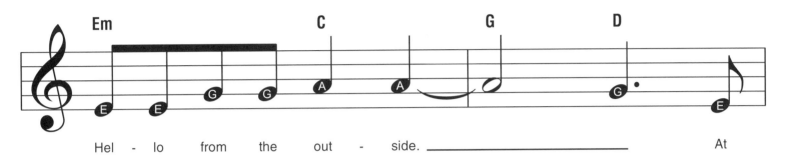

Hel - lo from the out - side. _____ At

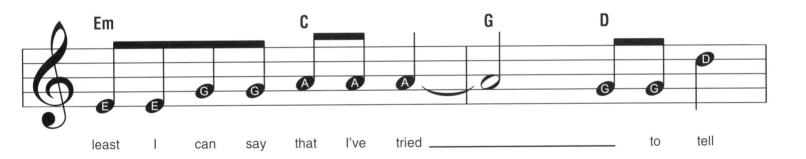

least I can say that I've tried _____ to tell

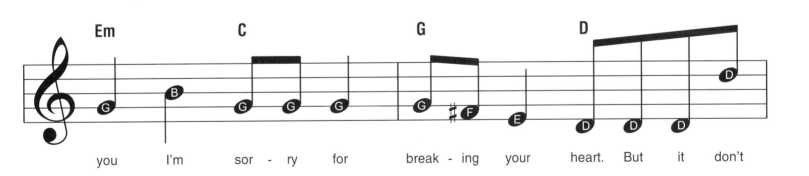

you I'm sor - ry for break - ing your heart. But it don't

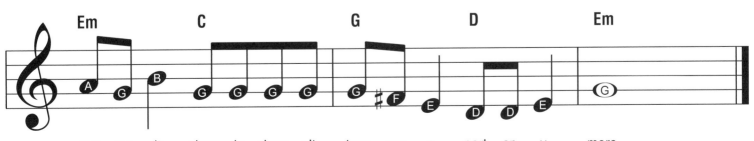

mat - ter. It clear - ly does - n't tear you a - part an - y - more.

Hometown Glory

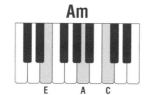
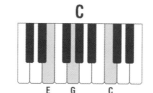
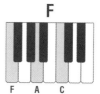

Words and Music by
Adele Adkins

Moderate half-time Ballad

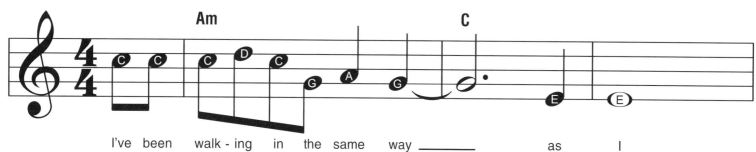

I've been walk - ing in the same way _____ as I

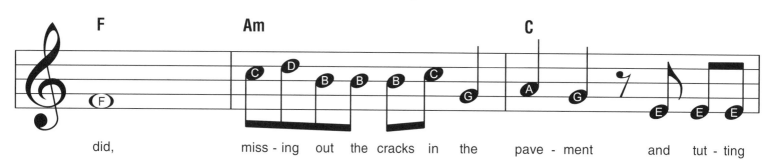

did, miss - ing out the cracks in the pave - ment and tut - ting

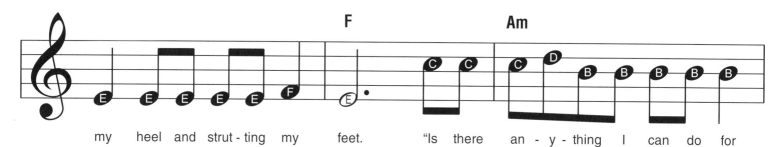

my heel and strut - ting my feet. "Is there an - y - thing I can do for

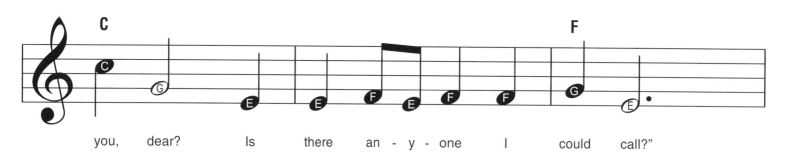

you, dear? Is there an - y - one I could call?"

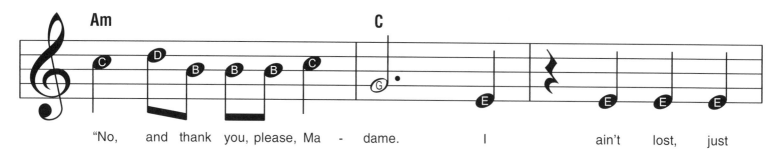

"No, and thank you, please, Ma - dame. I ain't lost, just

Lovesong

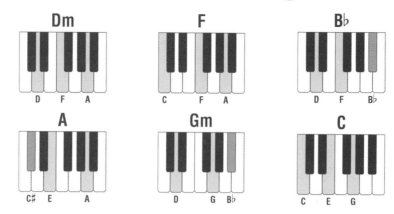

Words and Music by Robert Smith,
Laurence Tolhurst, Simon Gallup,
Paul S. Thompson, Boris Williams
and Roger O'Donnell

Moderate Ballad

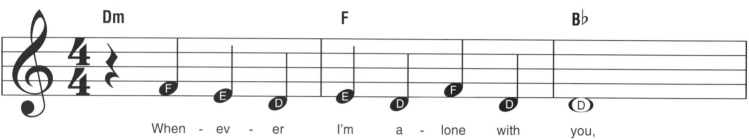

When - ev - er I'm a - lone with you,

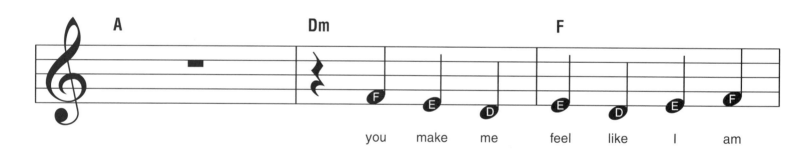

you make me feel like I am

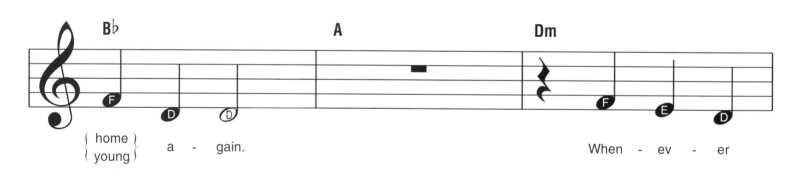

{ home }
{ young } a - gain.   When - ev - er

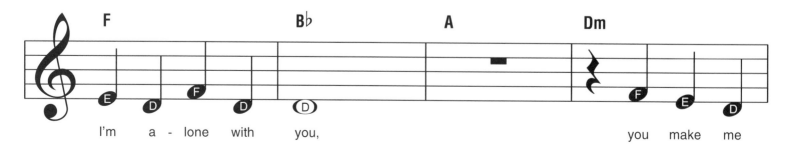

I'm a - lone with you,   you make me

21

Make You Feel My Love

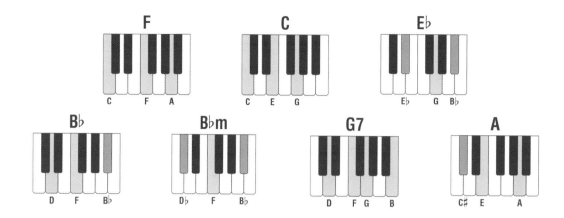

Words and Music by
Bob Dylan

Moderate Ballad

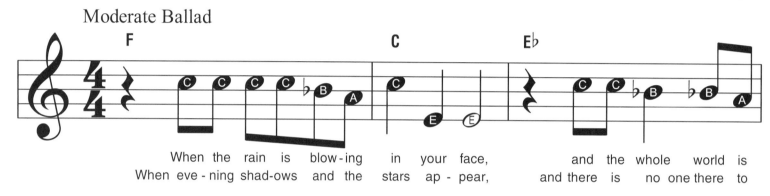

When the rain is blow-ing in your face, and the whole world is
When eve-ning shad-ows and the stars ap-pear, and there is no one there to

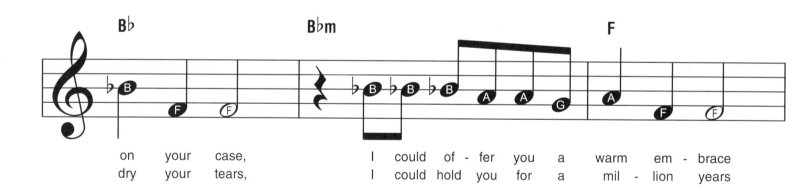

on your case, I could of-fer you a warm em-brace
dry your tears, I could hold you for a mil-lion years

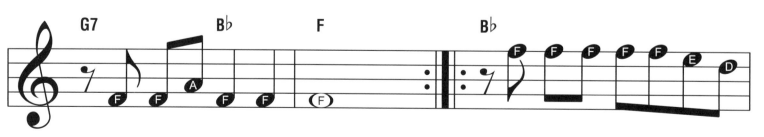

to make you feel my love.
to make you feel my love.

I know you have-n't made your
The storms are rag-ing on the

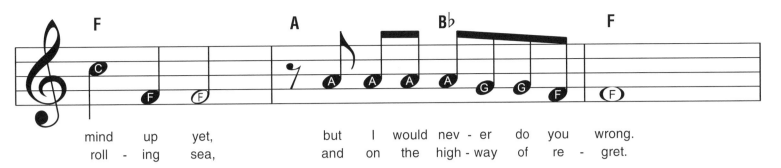

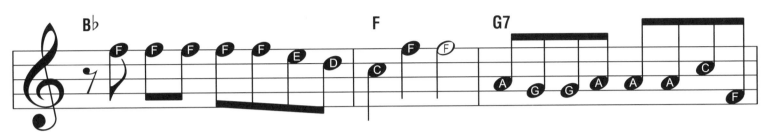

mind up yet, but I would nev-er do you wrong.
roll-ing sea, and on the high-way of re-gret.

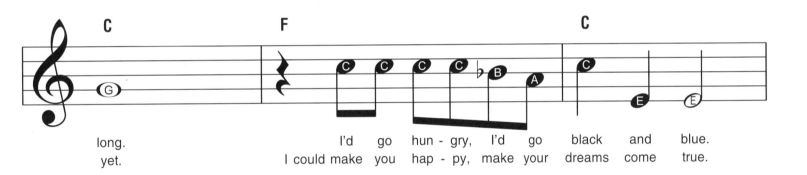

I've known it from the mo-ment that we met. No doubt in my mind where you be-
The winds of change are blow-ing wild and free. You ain't ___ seen noth-ing like me

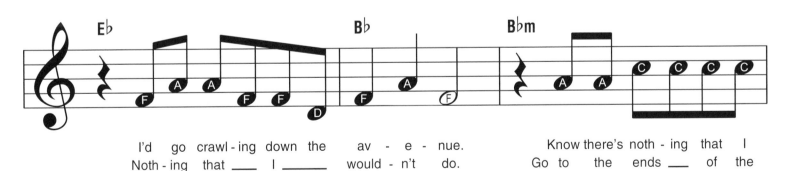

long.
yet. I'd go hun-gry, I'd go black and blue.
I could make you hap-py, make your dreams come true.

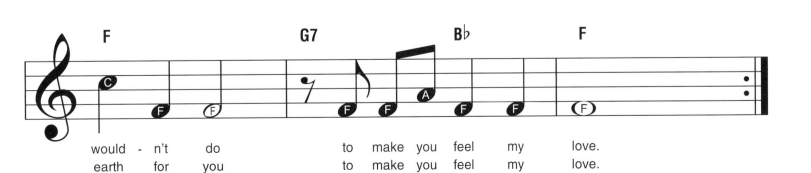

I'd go crawl-ing down the av-e-nue. Know there's noth-ing that I
Noth-ing that ___ I ___ would-n't do. Go to the ends ___ of the

would-n't do to make you feel my love.
earth for you to make you feel my love.

Oh My God

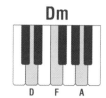
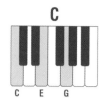
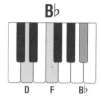

Words and Music by Adele Adkins
and Greg Kurstin

Moderate Shuffle

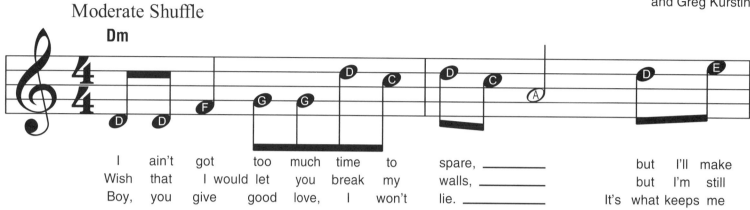

I ain't got too much time to spare, _____ but I'll make
Wish that I would let you break my walls, _____ but I'm still
Boy, you give good love, I won't lie. _____ It's what keeps me

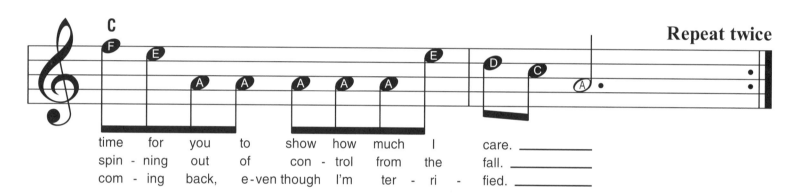

time for you to show how much I care. _____
spin-ning out of con-trol from the fall. _____
com-ing back, e-ven though I'm ter-ri-fied. _____

Repeat twice

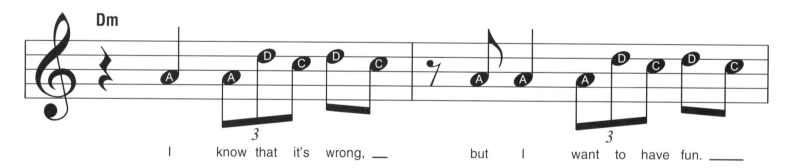

I know that it's wrong, ___ but I want to have fun. _____

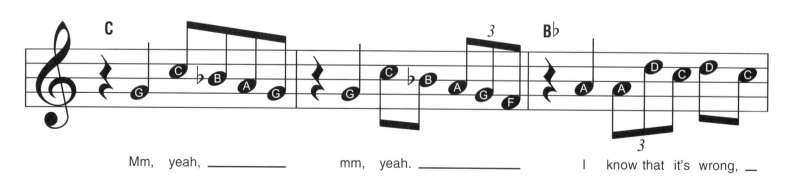

Mm, yeah, _____ mm, yeah. _____ I know that it's wrong, ___

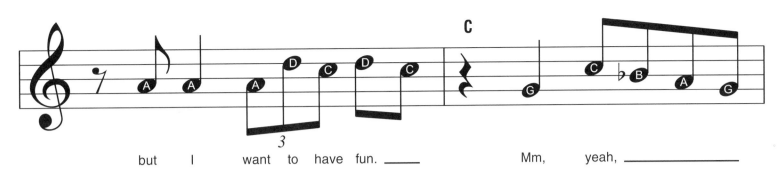

but I want to have fun. ____ Mm, yeah, _____

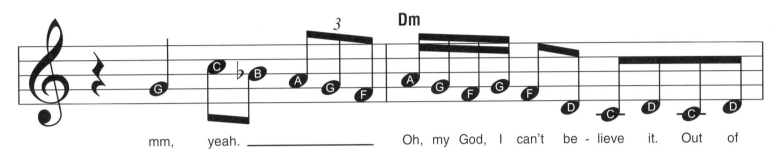

mm, yeah. _____ Oh, my God, I can't be - lieve it. Out of

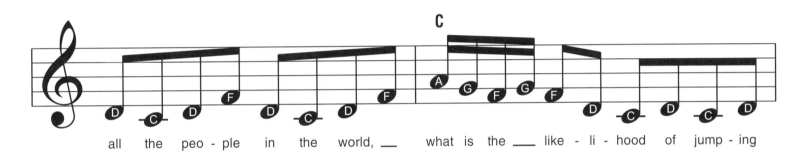

all the peo - ple in the world, ___ what is the ___ like - li - hood of jump - ing

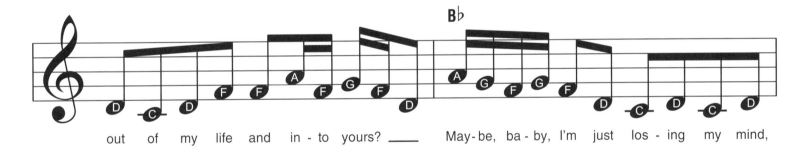

out of my life and in - to yours? ____ May - be, ba - by, I'm just los - ing my mind,

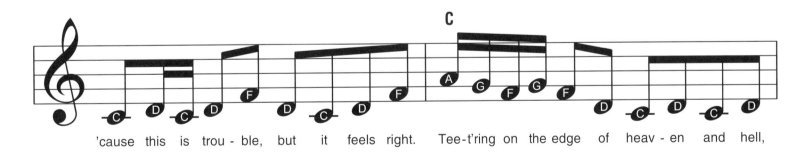

'cause this is trou - ble, but it feels right. Tee-t'ring on the edge of heav - en and hell,

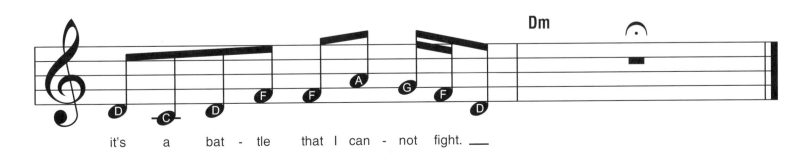

it's a bat - tle that I can - not fight. ___

One and Only

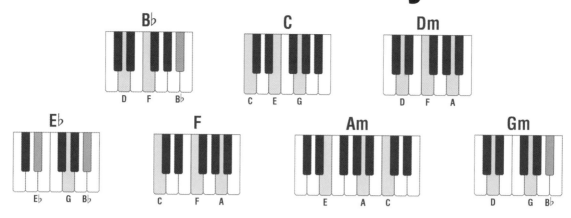

Words and Music by Adele Adkins,
Dan Wilson and Greg Wells

Moderately slow

I don't know why I'm scared; __ I've been here be-fore. __ Ev-'ry feel-ing,

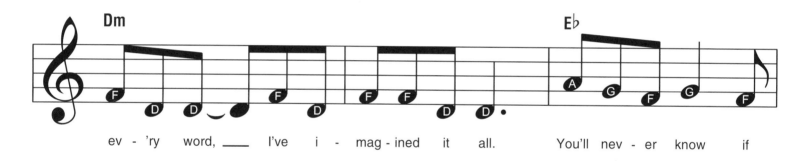

ev-'ry word, __ I've i-mag-ined it all. You'll nev-er know if

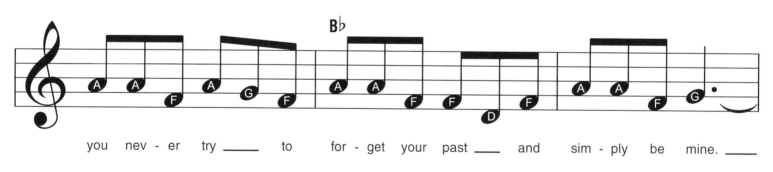

you nev-er try __ to for-get your past __ and sim-ply be mine. __

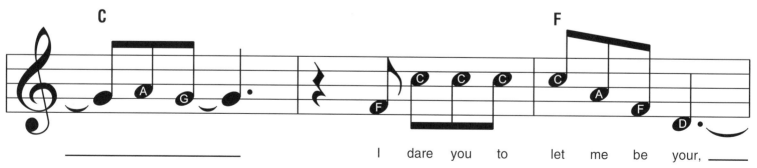

I dare you to let me be your, __

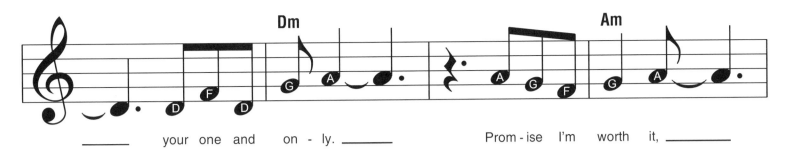

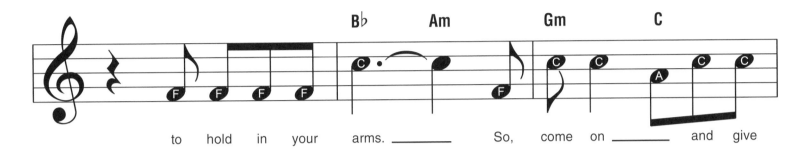

_____ your one and on - ly. _____ Prom - ise I'm worth it, _____

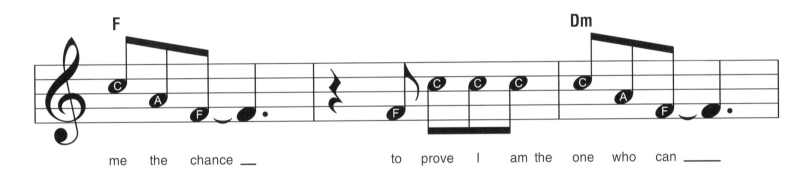

to hold in your arms. _____ So, come on _____ and give

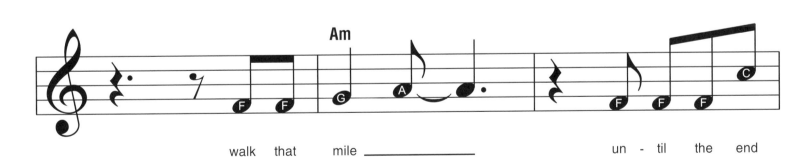

me the chance __ to prove I am the one who can _____

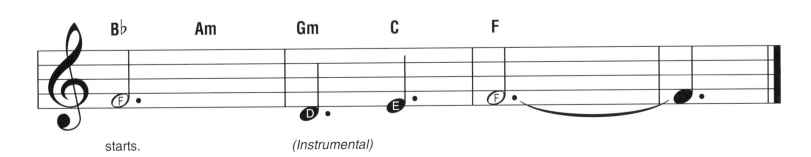

walk that mile _____ un - til the end

starts.   *(Instrumental)*

Remedy

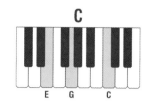
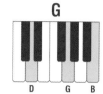
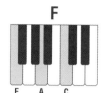
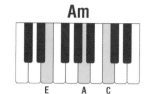

Words and Music by Adele Adkins
and Ryan Tedder

Flowing Ballad

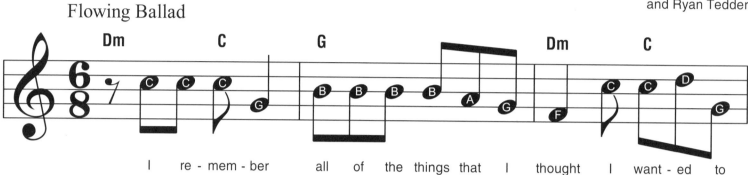

I re-mem-ber all of the things that I thought I want-ed to

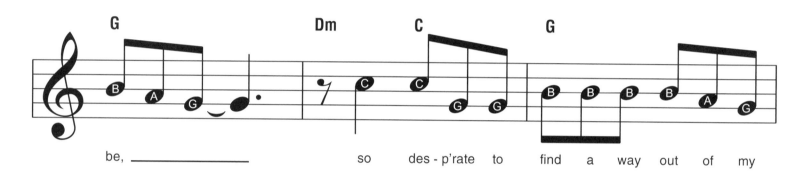

be, _____ so des-p'rate to find a way out of my

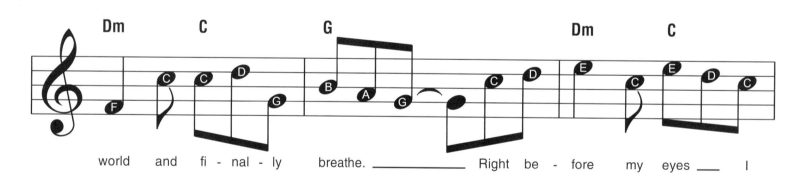

world and fi-nal-ly breathe. _____ Right be-fore my eyes ___ I

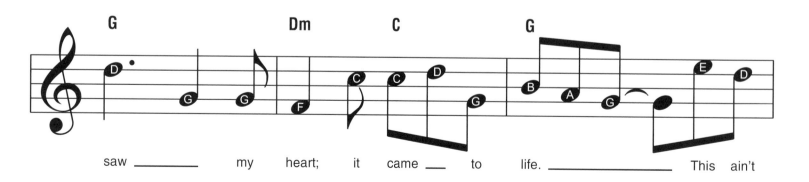

saw _____ my heart; it came ___ to life. _____ This ain't

(Instrumental)

Rolling in the Deep

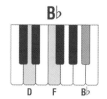
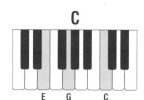
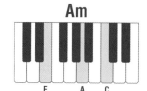
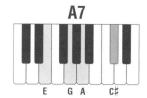
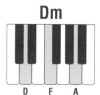

Words and Music by Adele Adkins
and Paul Epworth

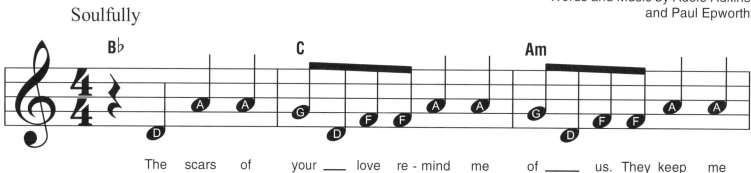

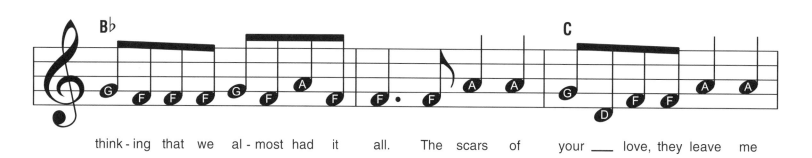

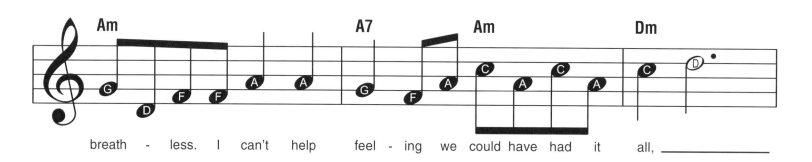

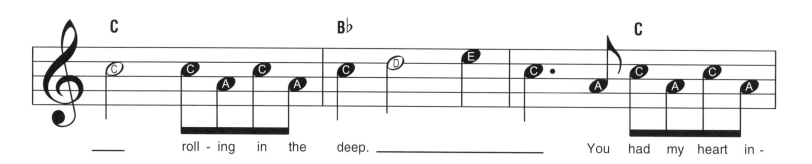

Rumour Has It

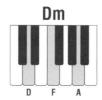
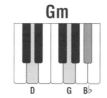
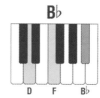

Words and Music by Adele Adkins
and Ryan Tedder

Moderately fast Rock

She,   she ain't real.   She ain't gon' be a - ble to love you like I

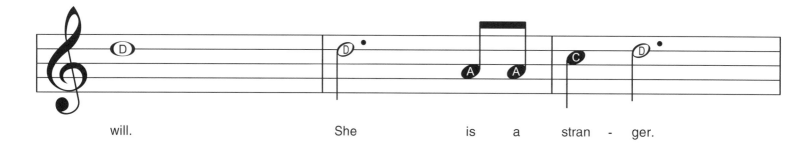

will.   She   is a stran - ger.

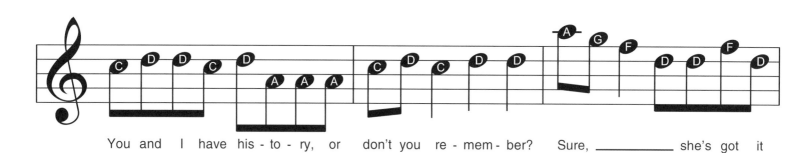

You and I have his - to - ry, or don't you re - mem - ber? Sure,   she's got it

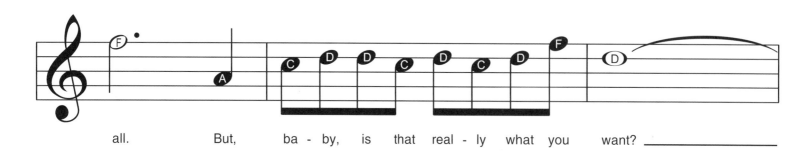

all.   But, ba - by, is that real - ly what you want? _____

Send My Love
(To Your New Lover)

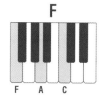
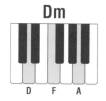

Words and Music by Adele Adkins,
Max Martin and Shellback

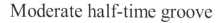
Moderate half-time groove

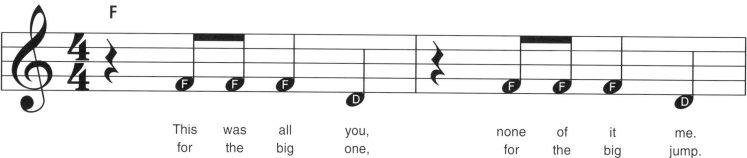

This was all you, none of it me.
for the big one, for the big jump.

You put your hands on, ___ on my bod - y and told _____ me,
I'd be your last love, __ ev - er - last - ing. ___ You _____ and me,

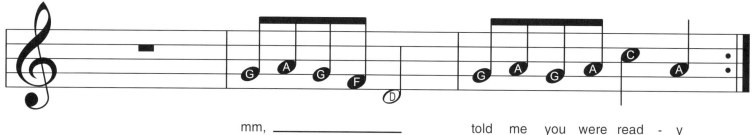

mm, _____
mm, _____

told me you were read - y
that was what you told me.

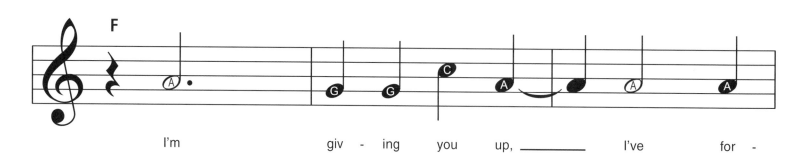

I'm giv - ing you up, _____ I've for -

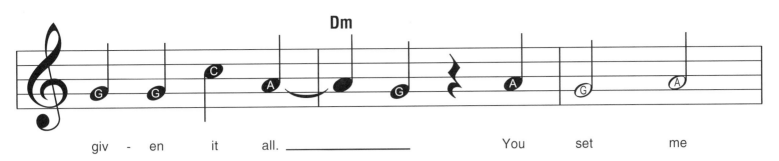

giv - en it all. _____ You set me

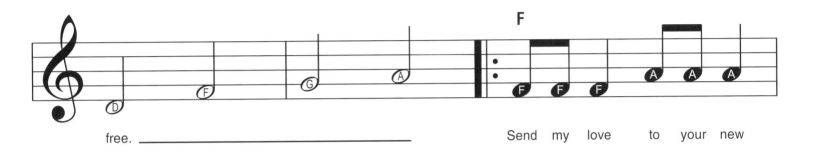

free. _____ Send my love to your new

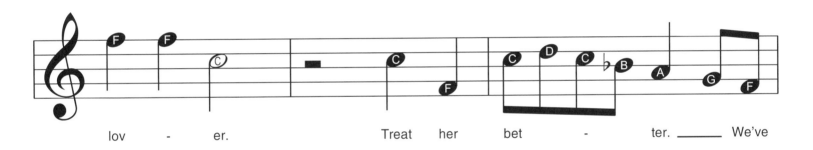

lov - er. Treat her bet - ter. _____ We've

got - ta let go of all of our ghosts. ___ We both know we ain't

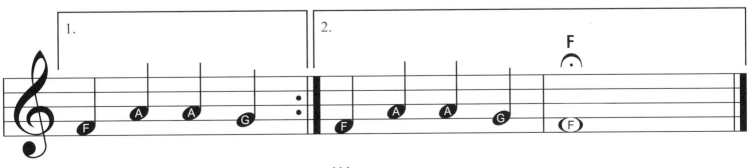

1. kids no more. _____ 2. kids no more. _____

Set Fire to the Rain

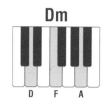 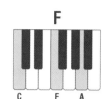 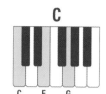  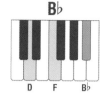

Words and Music by Adele Adkins
and Fraser Smith

I let it fall, my heart, and as it fell, you rose to claim _ it. It was dark, and I was o - ver _____ un - til you kissed my lips and you saved me. My hands, they were strong, but my knees were far too weak _____ to stand in your arms with - out fall - ing to your feet. _

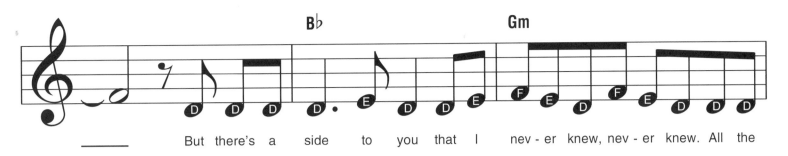

But there's a side to you that I nev - er knew, nev - er knew. All the

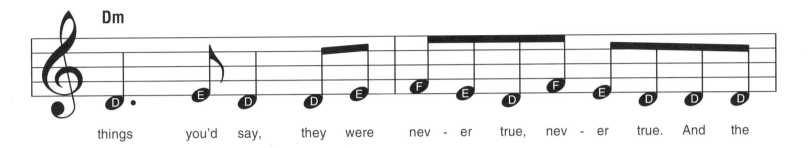

things you'd say, they were nev - er true, nev - er true. And the

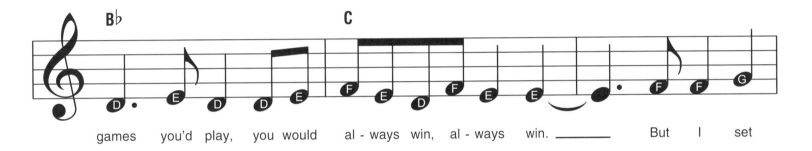

games you'd play, you would al - ways win, al - ways win. _____ But I set

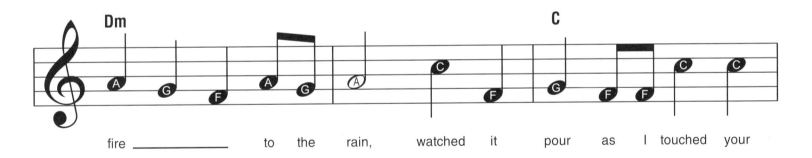

fire _____ to the rain, watched it pour as I touched your

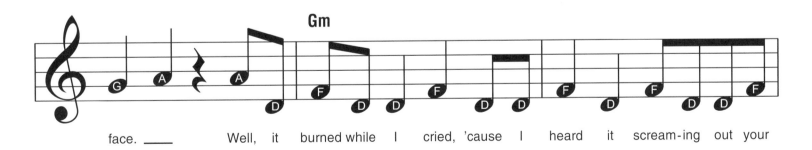

face. ___ Well, it burned while I cried, 'cause I heard it scream-ing out your

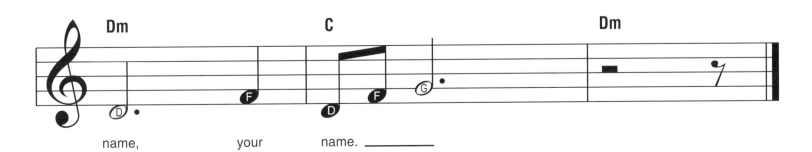

name, your name. _____

Skyfall
from the Motion Picture SKYFALL

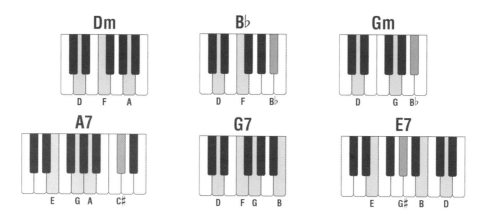

Words and Music by Adele Adkins
and Paul Epworth

Moderately

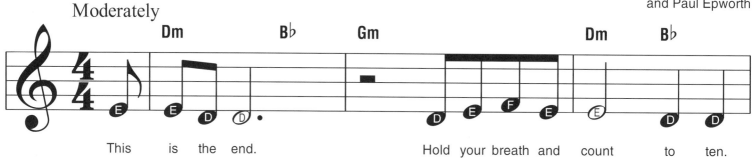

This is the end.   Hold your breath and count to ten.

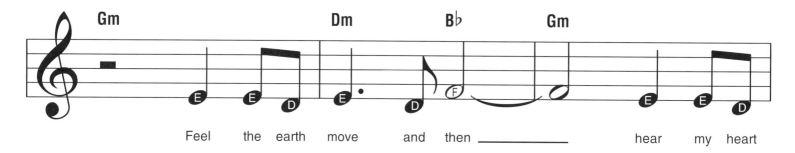

Feel the earth move and then _____ hear my heart

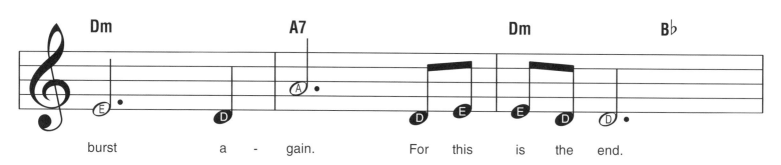

burst a - gain.   For this is the end.

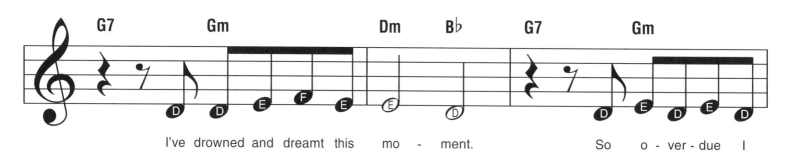

I've drowned and dreamt this mo - ment.   So o - ver - due I

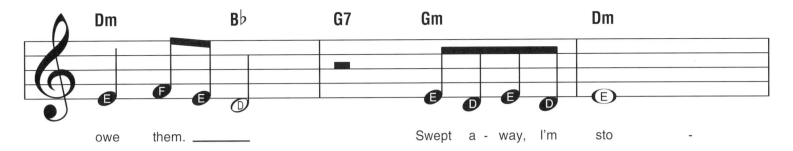

owe them. _____ Swept a - way, I'm sto -

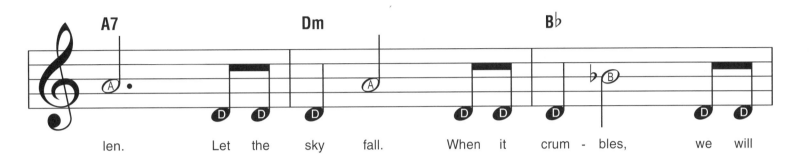

len. Let the sky fall. When it crum - bles, we will

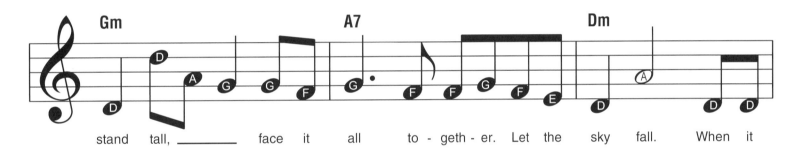

stand tall, _____ face it all to - geth - er. Let the sky fall. When it

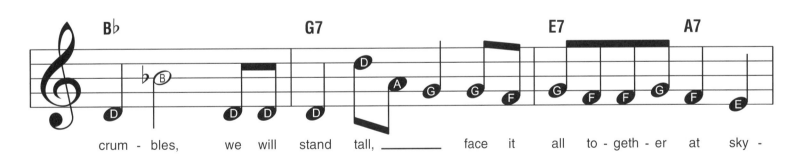

crum - bles, we will stand tall, _____ face it all to - geth - er at sky -

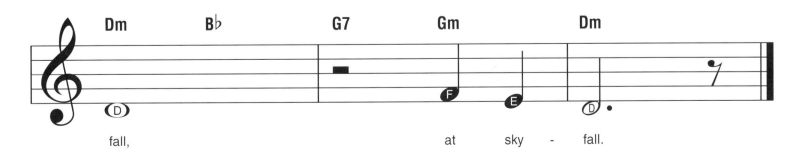

fall, at sky - fall.

Someone Like You

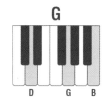
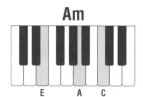
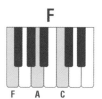
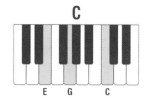

Words and Music by Adele Adkins
and Dan Wilson

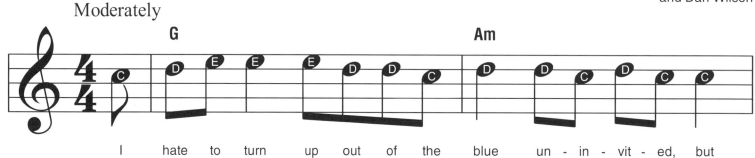

I hate to turn up out of the blue un-in-vit-ed, but

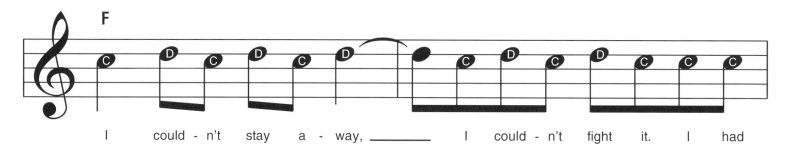

I could-n't stay a-way, _____ I could-n't fight it. I had

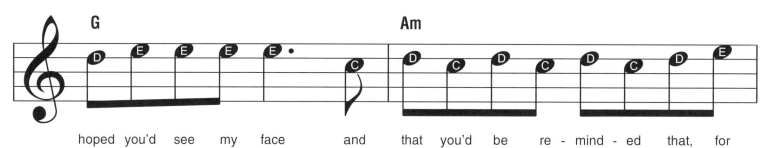

hoped you'd see my face and that you'd be re-mind-ed that, for

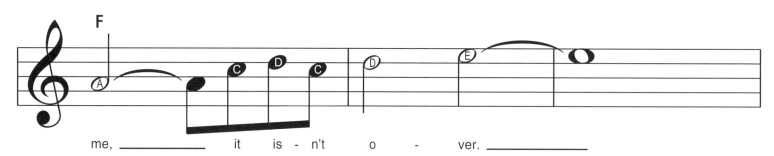

me, _____ it is-n't o-ver. _____

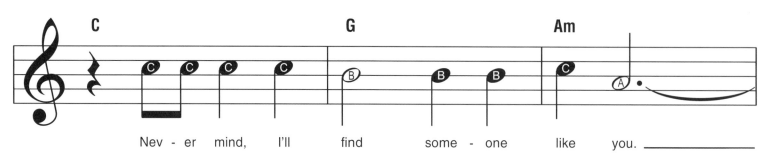

Nev-er mind, I'll find some-one like you. _____

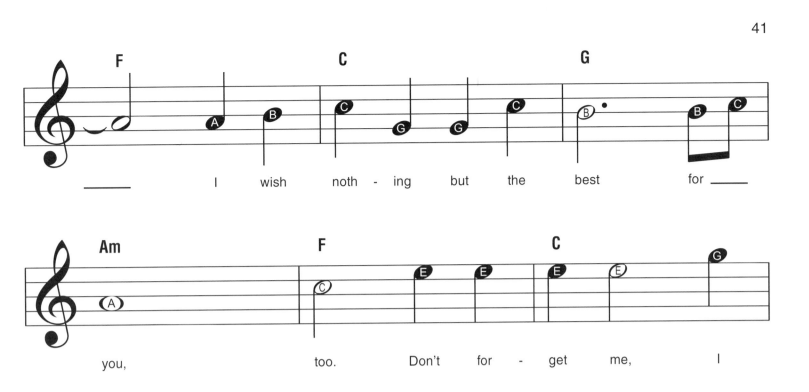

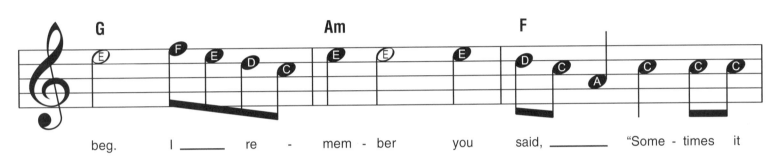

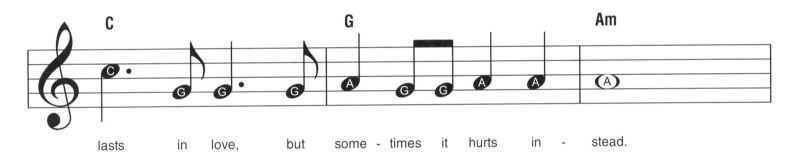

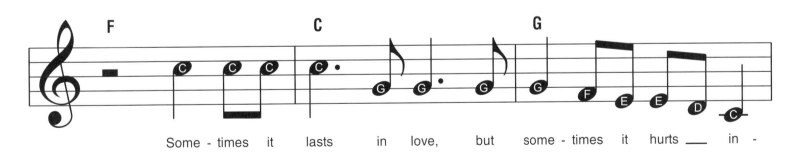

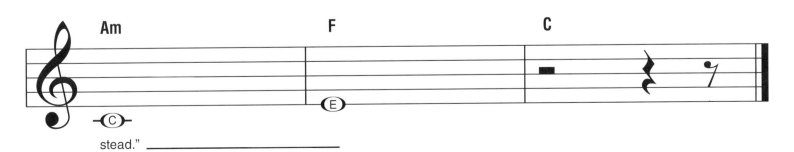

Turning Tables

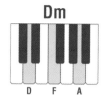 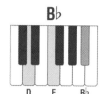  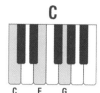 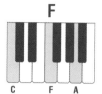

Words and Music by Adele Adkins
and Ryan Tedder

Moderate Ballad

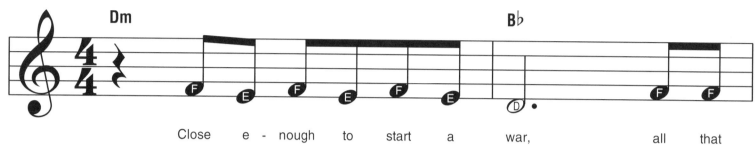

Close e-nough to start a war, all that

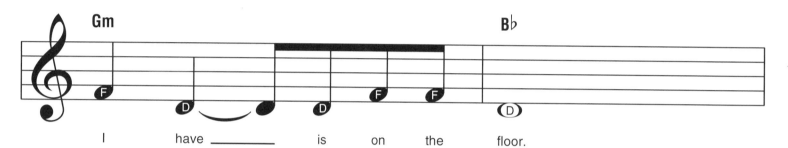

I have _____ is on the floor.

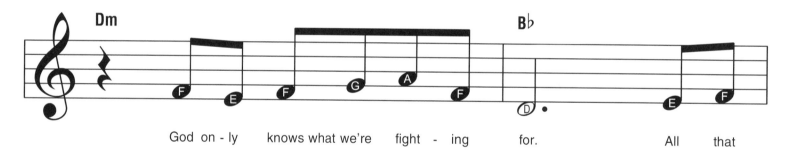

God on-ly knows what we're fight-ing for. All that

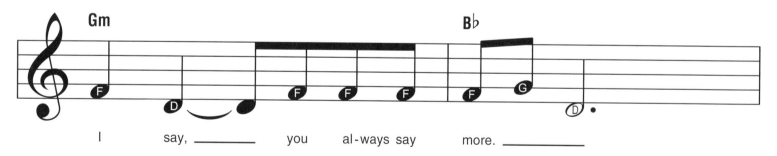

I say, _____ you al-ways say more. _____

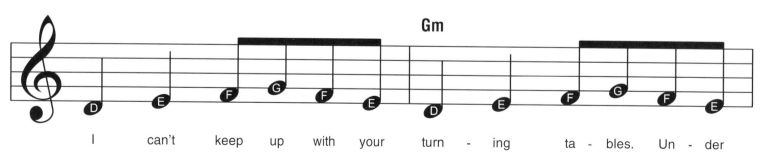

I can't keep up with your turn-ing ta-bles. Un-der

Water Under the Bridge

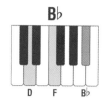
Bb

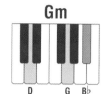
Gm

Dm

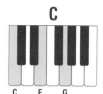
C

F

Words and Music by Adele Adkins
and Gregory Kurstin

If you're not the one for me,   then how
I'm not the one for you,   you've got-ta stop

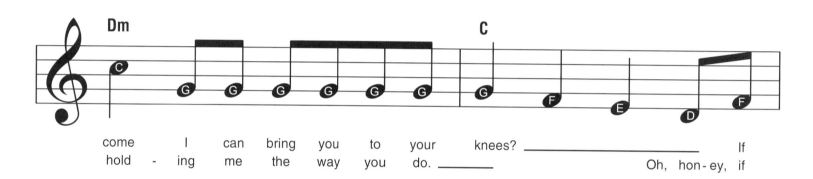

come I can bring you to your knees? _____ If
hold-ing me the way you do. _____ Oh, hon-ey, if

you're not the one for me,   why do I hate the i-dea of be-ing
I'm not the one for you,   why have we been through what we have been

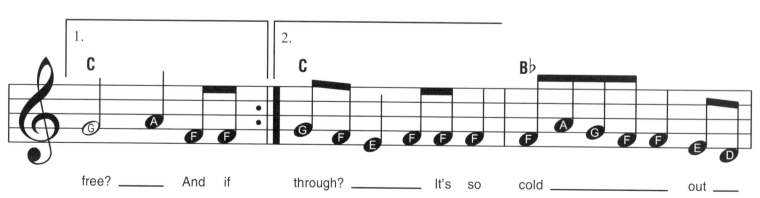

free? _____ And if   through? _____ It's so cold _____ out _____

here in your wil - der - ness. _____ I want

you _____ to be my keep - er, _____ but not if you are so reck-

less. _____ If you're gon-na let me down, let me down gen - tly.

Don't pre - tend that you don't want me. Our love ain't wa - ter un - der the

1.
bridge. _____ If you're gon-na

2.
bridge. _____ Whoa. _____

Say that our love ain't wa - ter un - der the bridge.

When We Were Young

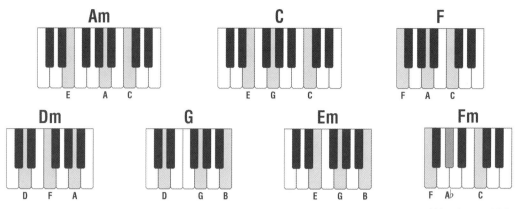

Words and Music by Adele Adkins
and Tobias Jesso Jr.

Moderate Ballad

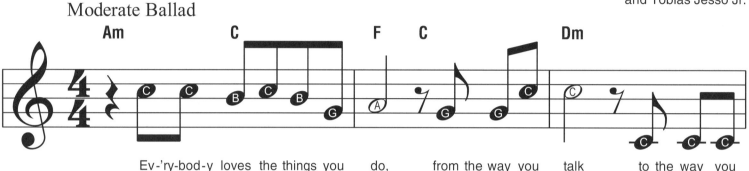

Ev-'ry-bod-y loves the things you do, from the way you talk to the way you

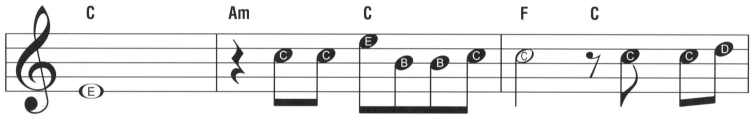

move. Ev-'ry-bod-y here is watch-ing you, 'cause you feel like

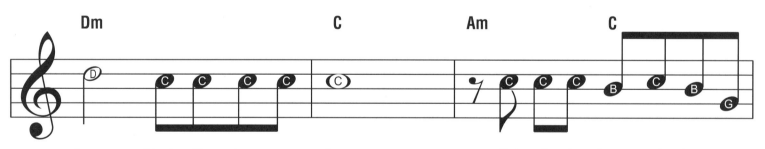

home. You're like a dream come true. But if by chance you're here a-

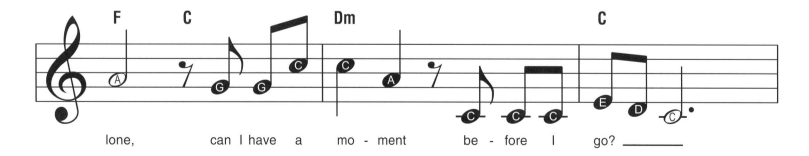

lone, can I have a mo-ment be-fore I go? _____

'Cause I've been by my-self all night long, hop-ing you're some-one I used to

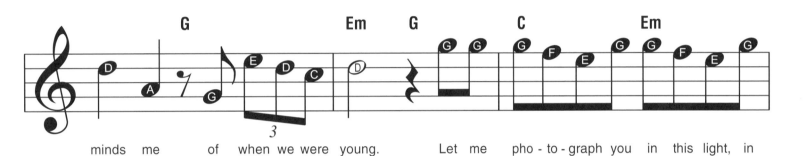

know. You look like a mov-ie, you sound like a song. My God, this re-

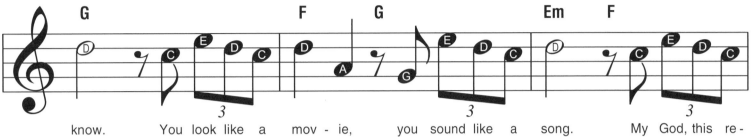

minds me of when we were young. Let me pho-to-graph you in this light, in

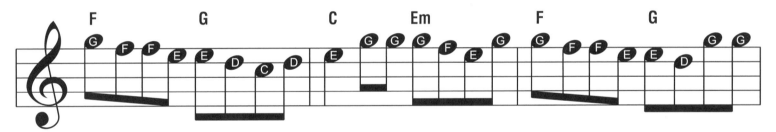

case it is the last time that we might be ex-act-ly like we were be-fore we real-ized we were

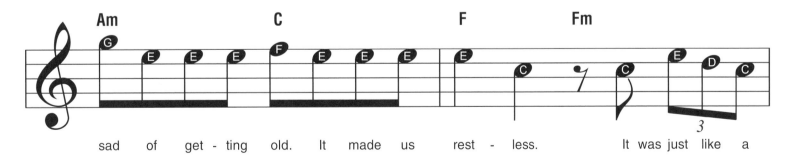

sad of get-ting old. It made us rest - less. It was just like a

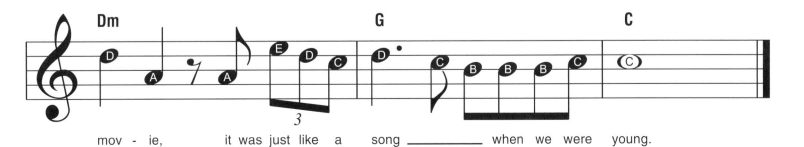

mov - ie, it was just like a song _____ when we were young.

SUPER EASY SONGBOOK

It's super easy! This series features accessible arrangements for piano, with simple right-hand melody, letter names inside each note, and basic left-hand chord diagrams. Perfect for players of all ages!

THE BEATLES
00198161 60 songs $15.99

BEAUTIFUL BALLADS
00385162 50 songs..........................$14.99

BEETHOVEN
00345533 21 selections $9.99

BEST SONGS EVER
00329877 60 songs..........................$15.99

BROADWAY
00193871 60 songs..........................$15.99

JOHNNY CASH
00287524 20 songs..........................$9.99

CHART HITS
00380277 24 songs..........................$12.99

CHRISTMAS CAROLS
00277955 60 songs..........................$15.99

CHRISTMAS SONGS
00236850 60 songs..........................$15.99

CHRISTMAS SONGS WITH 3 CHORDS
00367423 30 songs..........................$10.99

CLASSIC ROCK
00287526 60 songs..........................$15.99

CLASSICAL
00194693 60 selections..........................$15.99

COUNTRY
00285257 60 songs..........................$15.99

DISNEY
00199558 60 songs..........................$15.99

BOB DYLAN
00364487 22 songs..........................$12.99

BILLIE EILISH
00346515 22 songs..........................$10.99

FOLKSONGS
00381031 60 songs..........................$15.99

FOUR CHORD SONGS
00249533 60 songs..........................$15.99

FROZEN COLLECTION
00334069 14 songs..........................$10.99

GEORGE GERSHWIN
00345536 22 songs..........................$9.99

GOSPEL
00285256 60 songs..........................$15.99

HIT SONGS
00194367 60 songs..........................$15.99

HYMNS
00194659 60 songs..........................$15.99

JAZZ STANDARDS
00233687 60 songs..........................$15.99

BILLY JOEL
00329996 22 songs..........................$10.99

ELTON JOHN
00298762 22 songs..........................$10.99

KIDS' SONGS
00198009 60 songs..........................$15.99

LEAN ON ME
00350593 22 songs..........................$9.99

THE LION KING
00303511 9 songs..........................$9.99

ANDREW LLOYD WEBBER
00249580 48 songs..........................$19.99

MOVIE SONGS
00233670 60 songs..........................$15.99

PEACEFUL MELODIES
00367880 60 songs..........................$16.99

POP SONGS FOR KIDS
00346809 60 songs..........................$16.99

POP STANDARDS
00233770 60 songs..........................$15.99

QUEEN
00294889 20 songs..........................$10.99

ED SHEERAN
00287525 20 songs..........................$9.99

SIMPLE SONGS
00329906 60 songs..........................$15.99

STAR WARS (EPISODES I-IX)
00345560 17 songs..........................$10.99

TAYLOR SWIFT
00323195 22 songs..........................$10.99

THREE CHORD SONGS
00249664 60 songs..........................$15.99

TOP HITS
00300405 22 songs..........................$10.99

WORSHIP
00294871 60 songs..........................$15.99

HAL•LEONARD®
www.halleonard.com

Disney characters and artwork TM & © 2021 Disney

Prices, contents and availability subject to change without notice.

0222
327